What We Have in Common

A Brim Coloring Book

Written by Jane Landey
Edited by David Austin
Drawings by David Austin and Jane Austin

Published by CreateSpace: An Amazon Company.
Printed in U.S.A.

Introduction

What We Have in Common. Brim Coloring Books enable children to color the drawings as they read along! The books display the similarities of related animals. In this series, the horse and the zebra are compared. The facts enable children to appreciate common values. Thus, imbibing in them interest towards animals which could help them appreciate what they have in common with one another.

The Horse

And

The Zebra

The horse and the zebra have things in common. They are animals with tough bodies. They have thick skin and four limbs.

A horse and a zebra meet on a field.

I am a horse.

I am a zebra.

I have a mane.

I have a mane too!

I wear shoes.

I wear shoes too!

I have a long tail with fluffy hair.

So do I!

When it swings, the flies fly away.

When I swing my tail, flies fly away too!

I chew on hay.

I chew on curd too!

I can run and gallop.

I can run and gallop too!

I can drag wagons and chariots.

So do I!

I drink lots of water.

I drink lots of water too!

When I am angry, I kick.

So do I!

I am going to my stable.

Can I come along?

Yes you can!

Here we are!

This is beautiful!

Do you want some hay?

Oh yes! Does it taste nice?

It does!

How about this wood?

No, no, no, do not eat it!

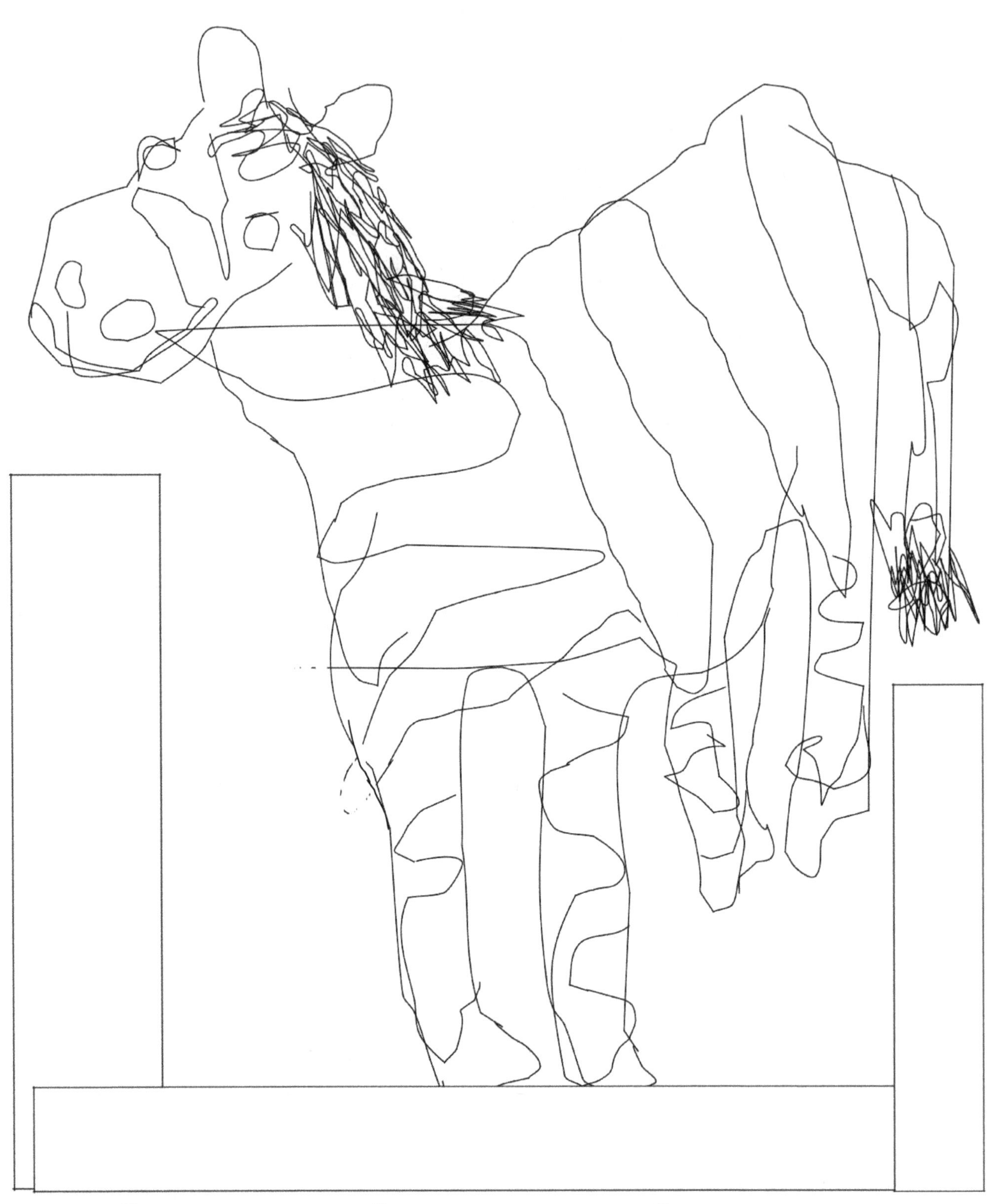

Because this is your home.

What We Have in Common Brim Coloring Books

Crocodile and Alligator
Turtle and Tortoise
Starfish and Octopus
Worm and Snake
Turkey and Vulture
Ostrich and Emu
Weka and Kiwi
Bat and Rat
Camel and Llama
Duck and Pelican
Kangaroo and Wallaby
Pig and Tapir
Skunk and Squirrel
Hedge and Anteater
Cat and Owl
Elephant and Rhinoceros
Dog and fox
Buffalo and Bull
Leopard and Cheetah
Horse and Zebra